Idaho Fish Species

Game Fish & Panfish

Billy Grinslott & Kinsey Marie Books

ISBN - 9781965098882

Chubs and Shiners are two types of minnows that are considered panfish. There are several types of shiners and chubs. Many people will use them as bate to catch larger fish. Here's a list of some. Bigmouth shiner, Emerald shiner. Golden shiner, Lake chub, Utah chub, Sturgeon chub, Roundtail chub

The Green Sunfish is blue green in color. It has yellow flecks on both its scales and some parts of its sides. The Green Sunfish also has broken blue stripes which is why some people confuse it with the Bluegill. Green Sunfish are very adaptable, they can live in any body of water that has vegetation or weeds.

Sculpins are small, bottom-dwelling fish with a flattened body shape, large pectoral fins, and a unique camouflage pattern, often found in clear, fast-flowing waters with rocky substrates, and they are known for their ambush hunting tactics. Sculpins have very large mouths and can swallow items nearly as large as themselves.

The burbot, also known as the eel pout. They get their name because they have a serpent-like or eel-like body. They can wrap their tail around things. There's nothing to worry about if you catch one, they may try to wrap their tail around your arm, but they are harmless. Burbots are adapted to cold water and are found in large, cold rivers, lakes, and reservoirs, primarily preferring freshwater habitats. Burbots are also known as eelpout, lingcod, and lawyer. The largest certified weight burbot (also known as lingcod) caught in Idaho weighed 14 pounds.

The bluegill also considered a sunfish is the most popular fish to fish for. They are called pan fish because they are about the size of a frying pan. Bluegills love to eat insects and bugs. They have good vision and rely on their keen eyesight to feed. Three types in this group are the Bluegill, Sunfish, and Pumpkinseed.

The Pumpkinseed is also known as pond perch, sun perch, and punky's sunfish. It can be found in numerous lakes, ponds, and rivers. It is their body shape resembling the seed of a pumpkin, that inspired their name. Pumpkinseed sunfish have speckles on their orangish colored sides and back, with a yellow to orange belly and chest. Pumpkinseeds can be found particularly in warmwater fisheries and other areas with similar habitats.

There are two main types of crapples. The white crappie and the black crappie. They are also members of the sunfish family. The difference between the white and black crappie is one has dark spots and the other has dark lines and is lighter in color. The white crappie has six dorsal fin spines, whereas the black crappie has eight dorsal fin spines. The white crappie can grow bigger and more of the bigger white crappie are caught in North America.

The Warmouth is a member of the Rock Bass, Green Sunfish and Bluegill family. They can survive in low oxygen environments while other fish cannot. Warmouth can thrive in muddy water, when other fish can't. Warmouth are often confused with rock bass. The difference between the two is in the anal fin: warmouth have three spines on the anal fin ray and rock bass have six spines.

Shad have exceptional hearing, including the ability to detect ultrasonic signals, which helps them navigate and avoid predators. Shad are energetic fighters and jumpers and have earned the nickname, the poor man's tarpon. Shad are anadromous, meaning they live in the ocean but migrate to freshwater rivers to spawn. The largest American shad ever recorded was two feet, six inches long.

The two most famous perches are the common perch and the yellow perch. The yellow perch has a brilliant greenish yellow color with orange fins. The yellow perch is the biggest one and can grow to a size of 18 inches. It's also known as the jumbo perch. The other type of perch is the white perch. The largest perch caught in Idaho, setting a new state record, weighed 3.22 pounds and was 16.25 inches long.

Northern pikeminnows are voracious predators, consuming millions of young salmon and steelhead annually in the river systems. They occupy a wide variety of habitats, including deep river channels, river shorelines, and slow-water sloughs. They are fast swimmers, capable of reaching speeds of 10 miles per hour. They can grow up to 35 inches in length and 15 pounds in weight and can live at least 11 years. The largest Northern pikeminnow caught in Idaho was a 27-inches.

Whitefish are related to salmon and trout. They are known for their deep-bodied, silvery appearance and are a major part of the lake's ecosystem. They typically grow to 17-22 inches and range from 1.5-4 pounds. Whitefish are a popular and valuable commercial fish, generating income for commercial fisheries. Whitefish are also known as, whiting, and shad.

The largemouth bass is the most sought-after bass in North America. Largemouth bass live in just about every lake in North America. They have great hearing and can hear a crayfish crawling on the bottom of the lake. The largest largemouth bass caught in Idaho weighed 10.94 pounds.

Smallmouth bass have a smaller mouth than the largemouth bass. They also have different markings and are lighter in color. They prefer living in colder water. They are typically found in the northern states in America because the water is cooler. The current world record smallmouth is an 11-pound, 15-ounce fish caught in Dale Hollow Lake. They can be found in lakes, reservoirs, and rivers. The largest smallmouth bass caught in Idaho, Weighed 9.1 pounds. Length was 23.75 inches.

Carp have long been an important food fish to humans. Carp are bottom feeders for the most part and their mouth is made like a suction cup, so they can suck food off the bottom. Carp are good for a lake because they help clean the bottom of the lake. Carp can tolerate a wide range of water temperatures and low oxygen levels, allowing them to survive in a variety of habitats. Carp are considered an invasive species in many areas. The largest carp caught in Idaho was a 46.7-pound grass carp.

The black bullhead and yellow bullhead are part of the catfish family. They usually only grow to about 10 inches long. They use their whiskers to help find food. The bullhead is the most common member of the catfish family. Bullheads live in the water containing low oxygen levels. They can survive on low oxygen areas, where other fish can't.

Flathead Catfish, their body is wide but flattened and very low in height. Both eyes are on the top of the flattened head, giving excellent vision to see upward. Flathead catfish live mainly in large bodies of water like big rivers and reservoirs. They prefer deep pools. The largest Flathead catfish caught in Idaho weighed 58.5 pounds and measured 48 inches.

There are several species of catfish. The Channel Catfish are the most fished catfish species with around 8 million anglers fishing for them per year. Channel Catfish have very few teeth and swallow their food whole. Channel catfish live in freshwater rivers, lakes, streams, and ponds. Catfish can live in low oxygen water, like bullheads. The largest channel catfish caught in Idaho, which was a blue catfish, was a 42.5-inch fish that weighed 37 pounds.

Sucker fish, also known as suckers, are freshwater fish with a unique sucker shaped mouth on the underside of their head. There are several types of sucker fish in Colorado. Sucker fish feed off the bottom with their suction cup shaped mouth. The official weight of the new longnose sucker record was 2 pounds, 4.5 ounces. The length of the fish was 18 inches.

Sturgeons have sharp spines on their back, so be careful when handling them. Instead of scales, sturgeon skin is covered in bony plates called scutes, which can be very sharp on young sturgeon. Sturgeons have been around since the dinosaur days. Sturgeons mostly live in large, freshwater lakes and rivers. Their average lifespan is 50 to 60 years. The largest white sturgeon caught in Idaho was a 10-feet, 4-inches long.

The sauger is part of the walleye family. There are 2 different types of saugers. The normal sauger and the suageye. The saugeye is a mix of the sauger and walleye. The suageye have white eyes just like the walleye. The sauger and suageye are smaller than the walleye. Saugers are more likely to be found in large rivers with deep pools but are also found in lakes. The largest sauger caught in Idaho weighed 8 pounds, 12 ounces.

The walleye got its name because of its white looking eyes. Their eyes collect light, even in low light conditions. This means they can see in the dark. Because they can see in the dark, they mostly feed at night. During the daytime their eyes are very sensitive, so they usually head for deeper water or shady places. Walleye like to live in cooler water and are normally found in the upper part of North America. They are found in various lakes and reservoirs. The largest walleye caught in Idaho, a state record, weighed 17 pounds, 14 ounces and was 34.5 inches long.

The Northern Pike is one of the most sought-after fish for anglers. It got its name because it likes to live in cooler water mainly in the northern states of North America. The northern pike is a very aggressive predator. They don't like to live in groups with other fish, they are very territorial and like to live alone. Their behavior is closely affected by weather conditions. Northern pike have eyes that can move in almost any direction. Northern pike can remain still for long periods of time. The largest northern pike caught in Idaho weighed 40.76 pounds, was 49 inches long.

Another breed of the Muskie is the tiger muskie. The tiger muskie is a cross between the northern pike and muskie. They grow larger and faster than normal muskies and northern pikes. The tiger muskie got its name because it has tiger like stripes. Tiger Muskies are very rare and hard to catch. The largest tiger muskie caught in Idaho, and a current state record, weighed 44.26 pounds and measured 52.5 inches long.

Mature Golden trout have a deep olive-green back that fades to bright gold on the sides, a vibrant red-orange lateral line, and black speckles near the tail. Golden trout are native to the remote waters at elevations of 6,000 to 10,000 feet. Golden trout, typically average 6 to 12 inches in length. The largest golden trout caught in Idaho, was a 19.7-inch fish.

The cutthroat's name comes from the bright red or orange slash-like markings under their jaws. There are several subspecies of cutthroat trout, including the coastal, Yellowstone, and Lahontan cutthroat. They inhabit a variety of cold, freshwater environments, including small streams, rivers, and lakes. Mature cutthroat trout can range from 6 to 40 inches in length. The largest West slope cutthroat trout caught in Idaho measured 25 inches long.

Bull trout thrive in cold, clean, and complex aquatic habitats, with water temperatures ideally below 55°F. Some bull trout are anadromous, meaning they migrate from freshwater to saltwater for part of their life cycle, and then return to freshwater to spawn. Bull trout usually grow to a common length of around 25 inches, with the maximum reported length being 40.5 inches. They are found in high-alpine lakes and streams. The largest bull trout caught in Idaho weighed 32 pounds, was 40.5 inches long.

Yellowstone cutthroat trout are distinguished by prominent red slashes on their lower jaws, large black spots, and orange to drab coloration. They inhabit relatively clear, cold streams, rivers, and lakes. They typically measure from 6 to 30 inches long when they reach maturity. The largest Yellowstone cutthroat trout caught in Idaho, and a new state record, was a 31-inch fish.

Steelhead are rainbow trout that migrate to the ocean and then return to their freshwater spawning grounds. Steelhead and rainbow trout are genetically identical, the difference lies in their lifestyle, with steelhead migrating to the ocean and rainbow trout remaining in freshwater. The largest steelhead caught in Idaho, and the current catch-and-release state record, was a41 inches.

Brown trout can live up to 20 years. Brown trout have higher tolerance for warmer waters than either brook or rainbow trout. Brown trout can be found on almost every continent except Antarctica, and many can be found living in the ocean. The largest brown trout caught in Idaho, according to the Idaho Fish and Game, weighed 27.31 pounds.

The rainbow trout gets its name because of its brilliant colors. Rainbow trout populations are good indicators of water pollution because they can only survive in clean waters. They like to live in rivers and streams. Rainbow trout rank among the top five most sought game fish in North America. The largest rainbow/cutthroat hybrid trout caught in Idaho was a 36-inch-long fish.

Brook trout are characterized by their olive-green bodies with pale, worm-like markings, red spots with bluish halos, and orange-red fins with white and black edges. They can grow up to 12 inches in length. Brook trout are cold-water fish that prefer clean, clear, and cold streams, lakes, and ponds. The largest Brook Trout caught in Idaho is a 21-inch, 7.06-pound fish.

The primary salmon species you'll find are landlocked sockeye salmon, also known as kokanee. These are the non-anadromous form of sockeye salmon, meaning they don't migrate to the ocean. They live their entire lives in freshwater lakes and reservoirs. The certified Idaho state record for a kokanee salmon is a 6.59-pound fish measuring 24.5 inches.

The Arctic grayling is one of the most beautiful freshwater fishes. Its most striking physical feature is the large, sail like dorsal or backfin. The Arctic grayling comes in a wide array of colors. Their color can vary from stream to stream. The sides of the body, fins and head can be freckled with spots. They can grow to be 30 inches long and weigh up to 8.4 pounds. They can travel more than 100 miles in one year. The largest Arctic grayling caught in Idaho measured 16.2 inches.

The lake trout is one of the biggest of the trout family. The biggest lake trout caught was 72 pounds. Lake trout like to live in lakes that are deep. They like being in the cool water in the deep parts of a lake. They have been reported to live up to 70 years in some Canadian lakes. The largest lake trout caught in Idaho was a 41.5-inch fish.

Coho salmon, also known as silver salmon, are fish that live in both freshwater and saltwater, migrating from the ocean to their natal streams to spawn, where they die shortly after. Some coho salmon migrate more than 1,000 miles in the ocean, while others remain in marine areas close to the streams where they were born. Adult coho salmon typically weigh 8 to 12 pounds and are 24 to 30 inches long, but some can reach up to 36 pounds. The largest coho salmon caught in Idaho was a 32.68-inch, 11.78-pound fish.

Chinook also known as the king salmon are the most widespread Salmon in North America. Chinook salmon are hatch in freshwater streams and rivers then migrate out to the saltwater environment of the ocean to feed and grow. Chinook salmon are the largest of the Pacific Ocean salmon, that's how they got the name king salmon. The largest Chinook salmon caught in Idaho weighed 54 pounds.

Fun Facts About Idaho Fish

1 - The cutthroat trout is Idaho's state fish, with three types found, the Yellowstone, West Slope, and Bonneville cutthroat.

2 - The white sturgeon, one of the largest freshwater fish in North America, some weighing up to 1,500 pounds.

3 - The burbot, or freshwater ling cod, is the only freshwater ling cod species in North America found on the Kootenai River.

4 - Idaho's native sport fish are mostly cold-water species, including trout and other salmon.

5 - The 425-mile Salmon River is the largest tributary of the Snake River and the longest free-flowing river in the lower 48 states.

6 - Salmon and Steelhead migrate 466 miles from the Pacific ocean to spawn in Idaho's mountain streams.

7 - The biggest fish caught in Idah was a 40.76-pound northern pike caught on Hayden Lake in North Idaho.

Author Page

Billy Grinslott & Kinsey Marie Books

Copyright, All Rights Reserved

ISBN – 9781965098882

Thanks

www.ingramcontent.com/pod-product-compliance
Lightning Source LLC
Chambersburg PA
CBHW060850270326
41934CB00002B/77